KINGFISHER
Larousse Kingfisher Chambers Inc.
80 Maiden Lane
New York, New York 10038
www.kingfisherpub.com

First published in 2002
2 4 6 8 10 9 7 5 3 1

1TR/1101/TIMS/FR(FR)/115OGPR

LIBRARY OF CONGRESS CATALOGING-IN-PUBLICATION DATA
has been applied for.

ISBN 0-7534-5433-5

Printed in China

Written by Ann Montague-Smith
Illustrated by Mandy Stanley

Editor: Jennie Morris
Designer: Jane Buckley
DTP Manager: Nicky Studdart
Production: Jo Blackmore

First Shape Book

KINGFISHER

NEW YORK

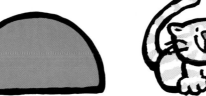

Suggestions for parents

Children soon learn that there are shapes all around them, but at first they cannot distinguish between the different shapes they see. Learning about shapes—their names, characteristics, and the similarities and differences between them—is a difficult skill to acquire. By familiarizing your child with two-dimensional shapes, this colorful and inviting book will be an invaluable aid to this process.

Very young children will enjoy browsing through the book and looking at the colorful pictures. Encourage them to talk about the shapes in the pictures, name the shapes, and ask your child to find other shapes that are similar.

When you look at this book together, make it an enjoyable experience. Encourage your child to talk about the shapes, and name them together. Point to other shapes and encourage your child to name these shapes too. Ask your child to describe the shapes: Do they have curved or straight sides? How many sides do they have? Ask them to seek out other examples in the book. Your child can compare the shapes and objects drawn on the page and match them. Encourage your child to compare the different shapes that

4

Contents

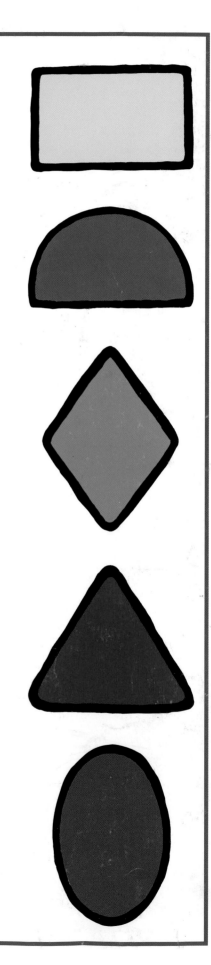

Now I know...

teddy bear

socks

mug

hat

47

ball

toothbrush

How many triangles can you count?

Who owns what?

What shape does the boy in the red hat like?

presents

sandwiches on a plate

candy

clown

How many circles can you see on the clown?

Find the shapes at the party

cakes

balloon

hat

drum

What shapes are the cakes?

airplanes

trucks

motorcycles

roller skates

Which is the largest motorcycle?

Big and small

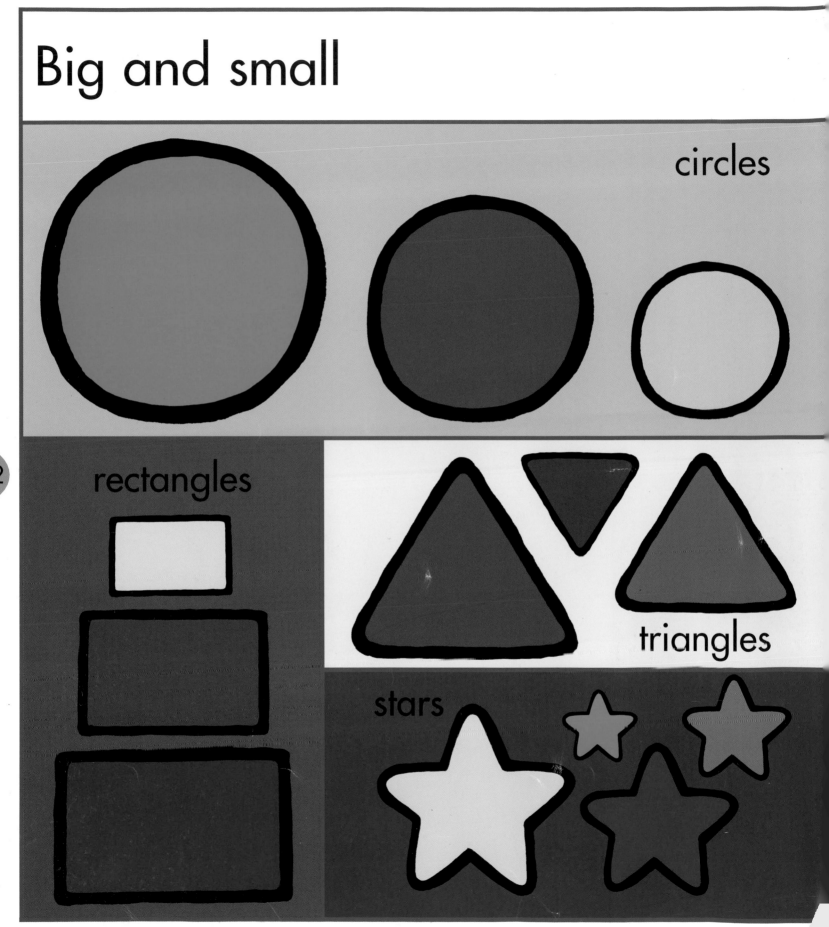

circles

rectangles

triangles

stars

42

Which is the smallest star?

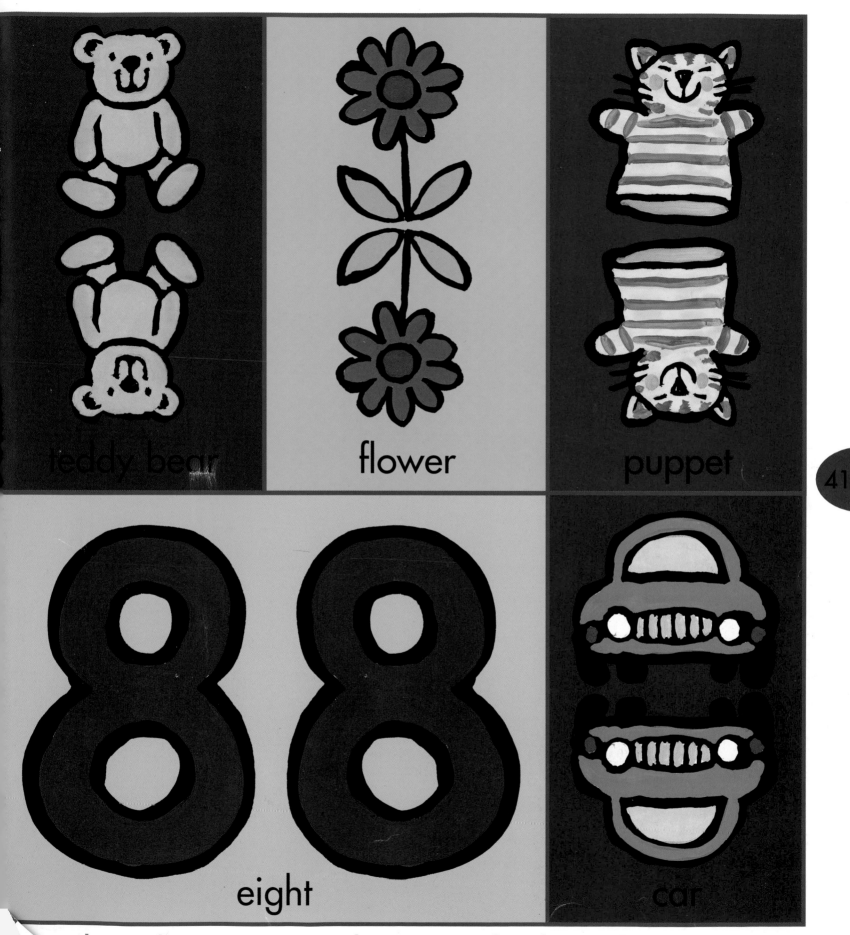

teddy bear

flower

puppet

eight

car

What do you see when you look in the mirror?

Look in the mirror

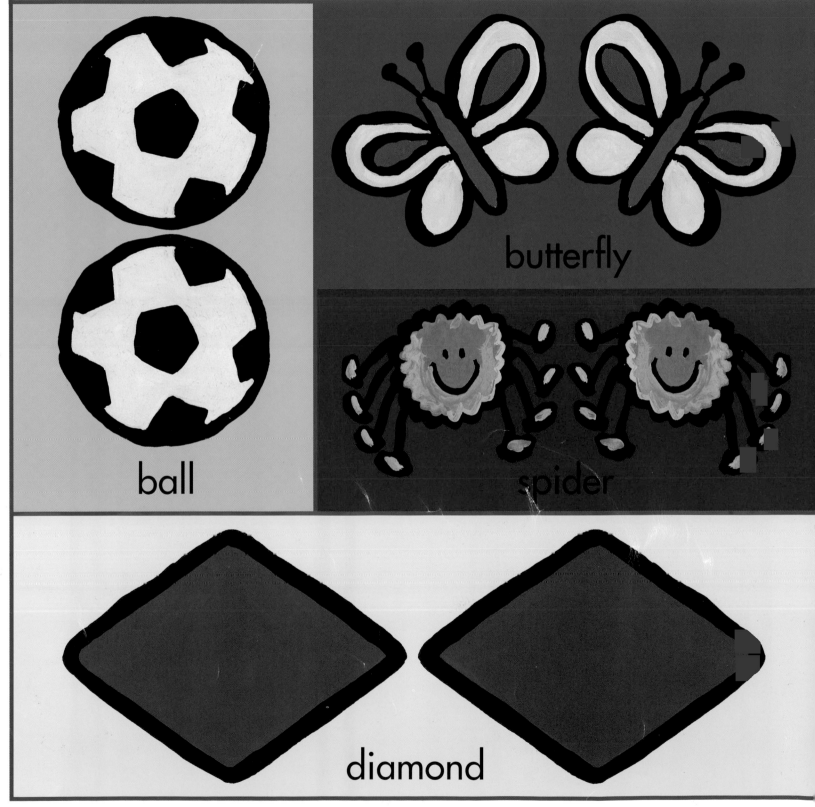

ball

butterfly

spider

diamond

Where would the mirrors be in each picture?

Can you make up your own pattern?

Spot the patterns

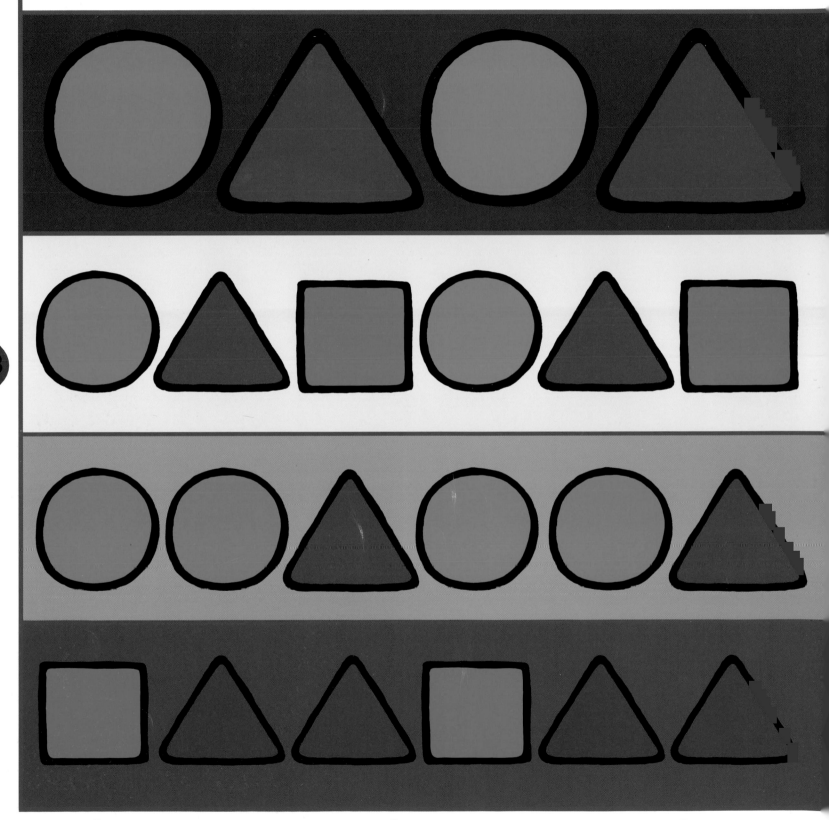

What comes next in these patterns? And next?

bed

leaf

cheese

tank

cushion

37

What shapes can you see in the tank?

Find the pairs

dog

fish

mouse

cat

caterpillar

36

What has each animal lost?

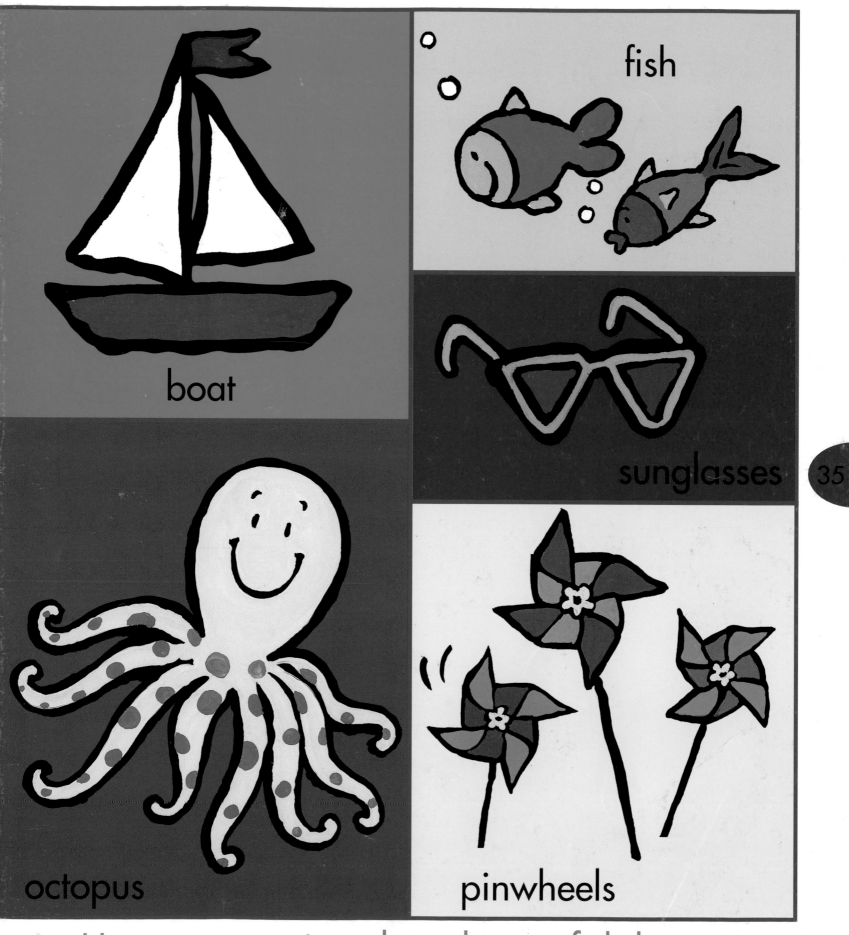

boat

fish

sunglasses

octopus

pinwheels

How many points does the starfish have?

Shapes at the beach

flags

ice cream

beach ball

starfish

Which shapes can you see?

What other shapes can you play with?

At the playground

Which shapes have curved sides?

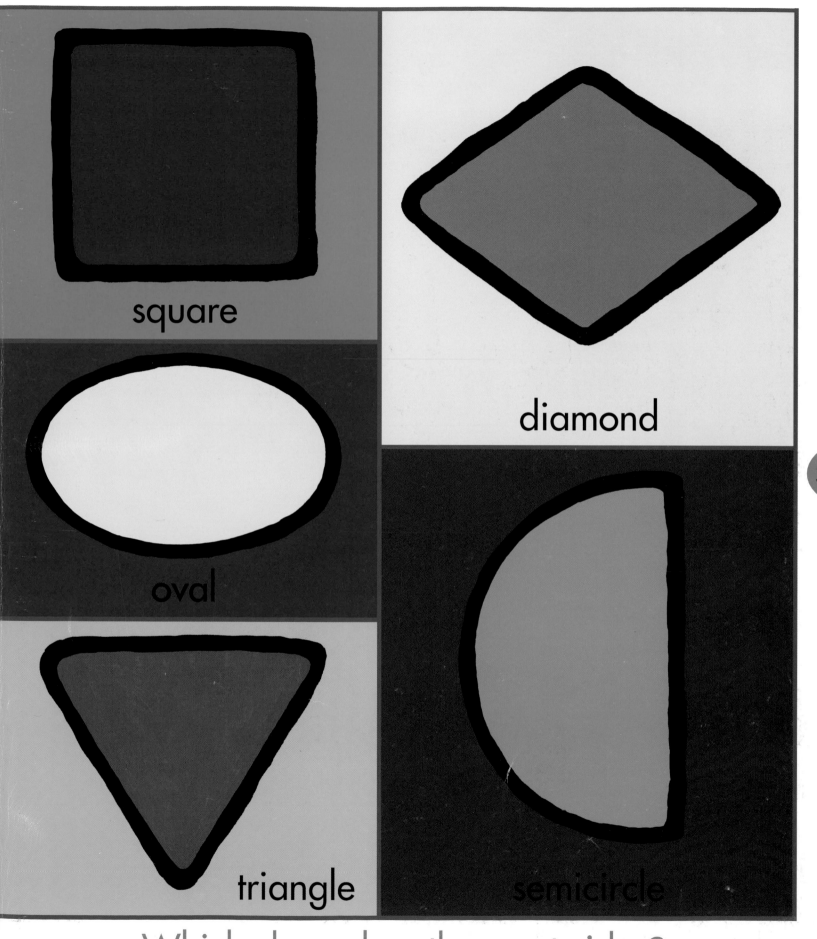

square

diamond

oval

31

triangle

semicircle

Which shape has the most sides?

How many sides do shapes have?

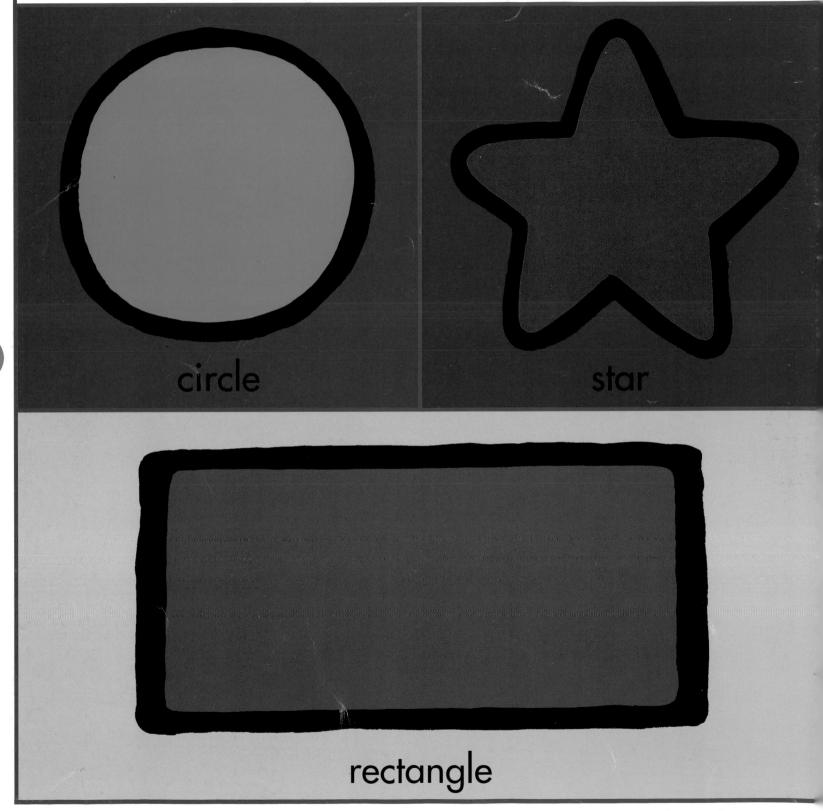

circle

star

rectangle

Which shapes have the same number of sides?

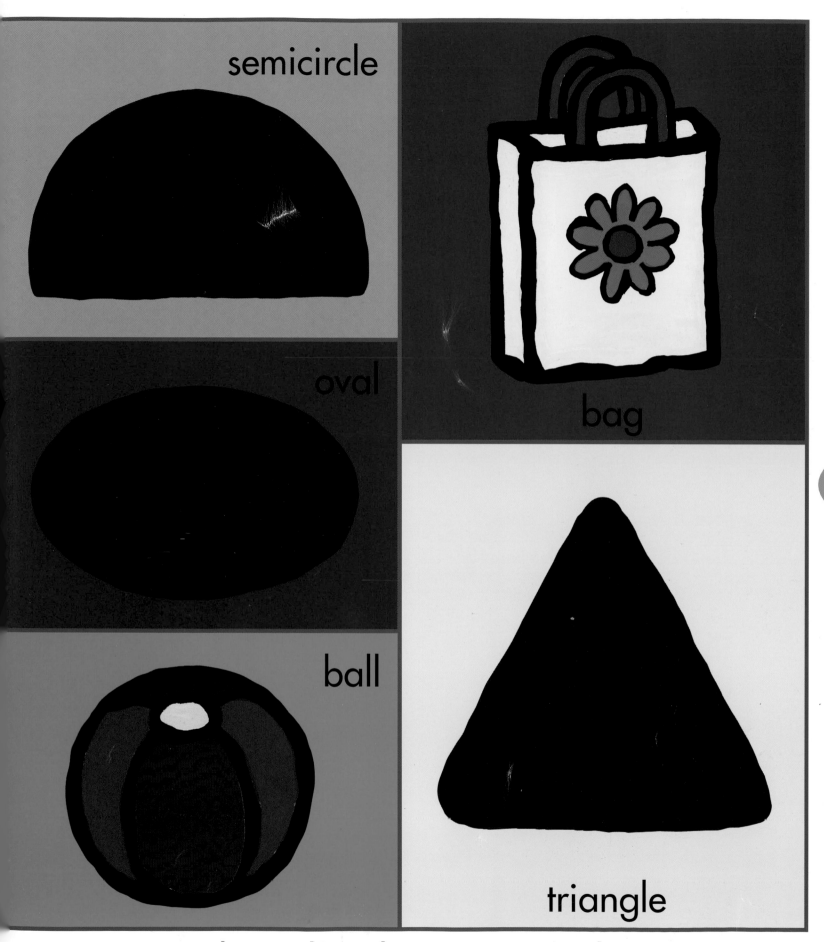

semicircle

oval

ball

bag

triangle

What other things are circles?

Match the objects to the shapes

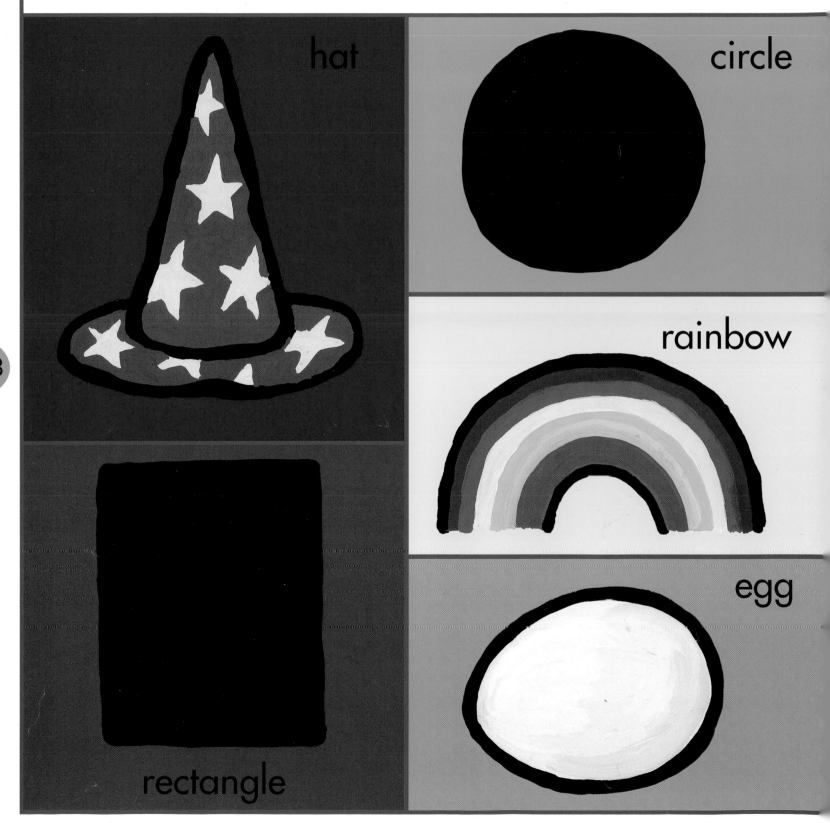

hat

circle

rainbow

egg

28

rectangle

What shape is the egg?

half a cake

half a lollipop

half an egg yolk

half a pizza

half a watermelon

Can you find a semicircle at home?

Circles and semicircles

lollipop

cake

egg yolk

pizza

watermelon

Which circles do you like to eat?

hairbrush

sink

pineapple

25

gem

zero

How many blue ovals can you see?

Ovals

oval

picture frame

leaf

face

Can you draw an oval?

diamond

kite

scarf

jockey

jewels in a crown

Can you draw a kite?

Stars and diamonds

star

star

flag

starfish

fairy's wand

What shape is on the flag?

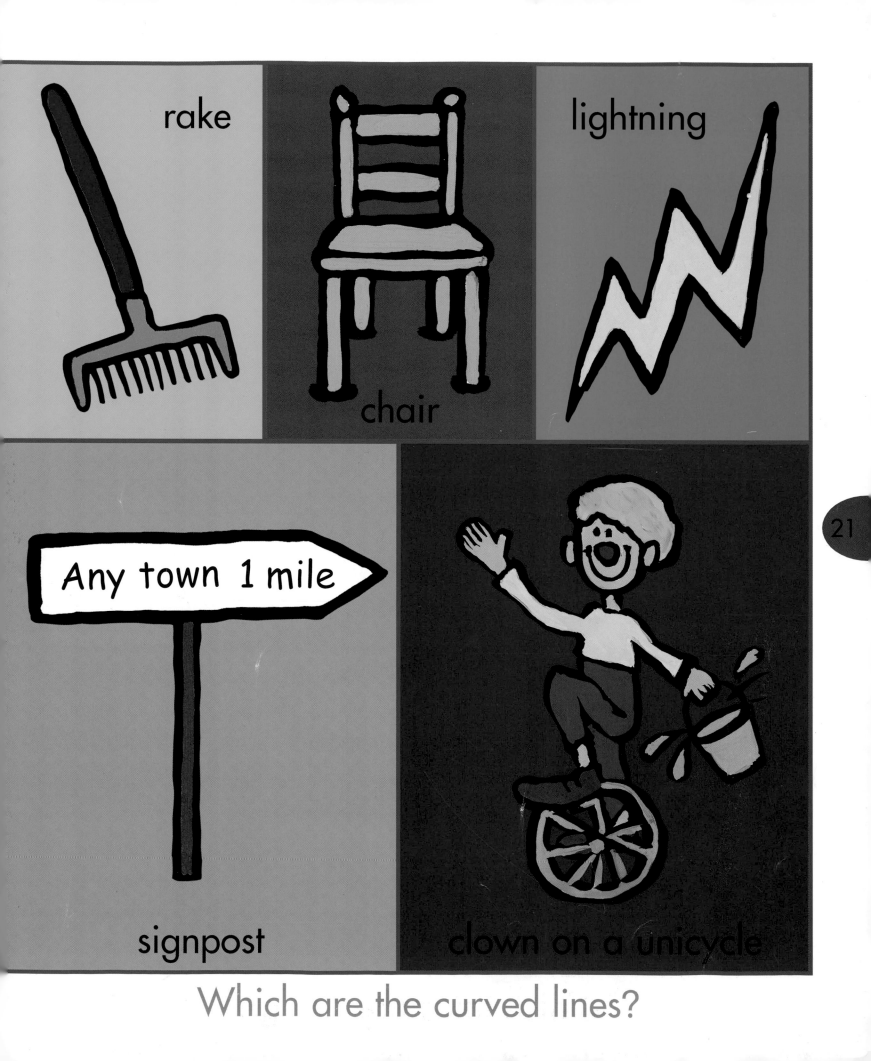

rake

chair

lightning

Any town 1 mile

signpost

clown on a unicycle

Which are the curved lines?

Is it straight?

pencil

one

seesaw

ladder

Which lines are straight?

seahorse

gymnast

snake

apple

9

nine

Which other numbers have curves?

Is it curved?

ball

banana

cat

hula hoop

Can you trace the curves with your finger?

boat

lollipop

17

window

door

How many rectangles can you count?

Look again

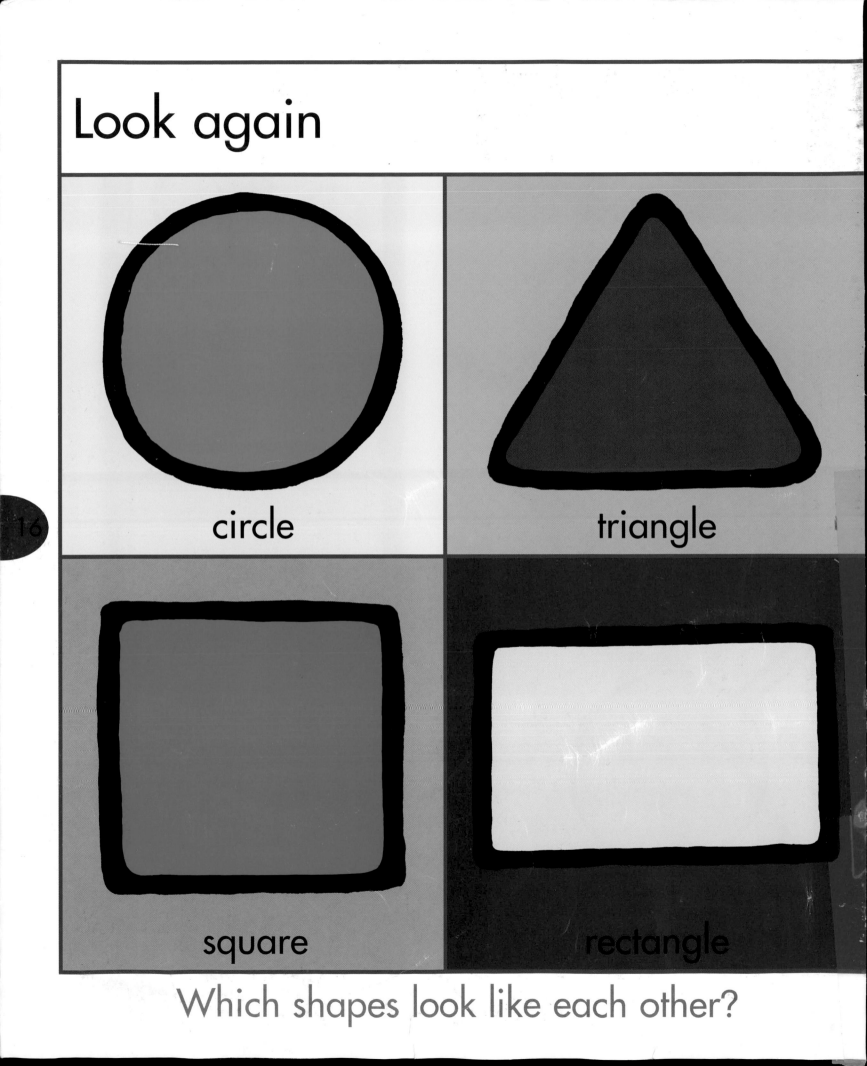

circle

triangle

square

rectangle

Which shapes look like each other?

crackers

bookshelf and books

television and table

sofa and cushions

Can you see any squares?

Rectangles

rectangle

playing card

birthday card

ruler

1
2
3
4
5
6
7
8
9
10
11
12
13
14
15
16

Which is the longest rectangle?

Come to my party

Sally

invitation

gate

1
2 3
4
5 6
7
8 9
10

hopscotch

What shape is the gate handle?

Squares

square

envelope

Mr. Eric Fisher

123 Harbor Lane

Seatown, ME 01234

window

bag

Can you draw a square?

flags

dinosaur's spikes

11

musical triangle

slice of pizza

Can you draw a triangle?

Triangles

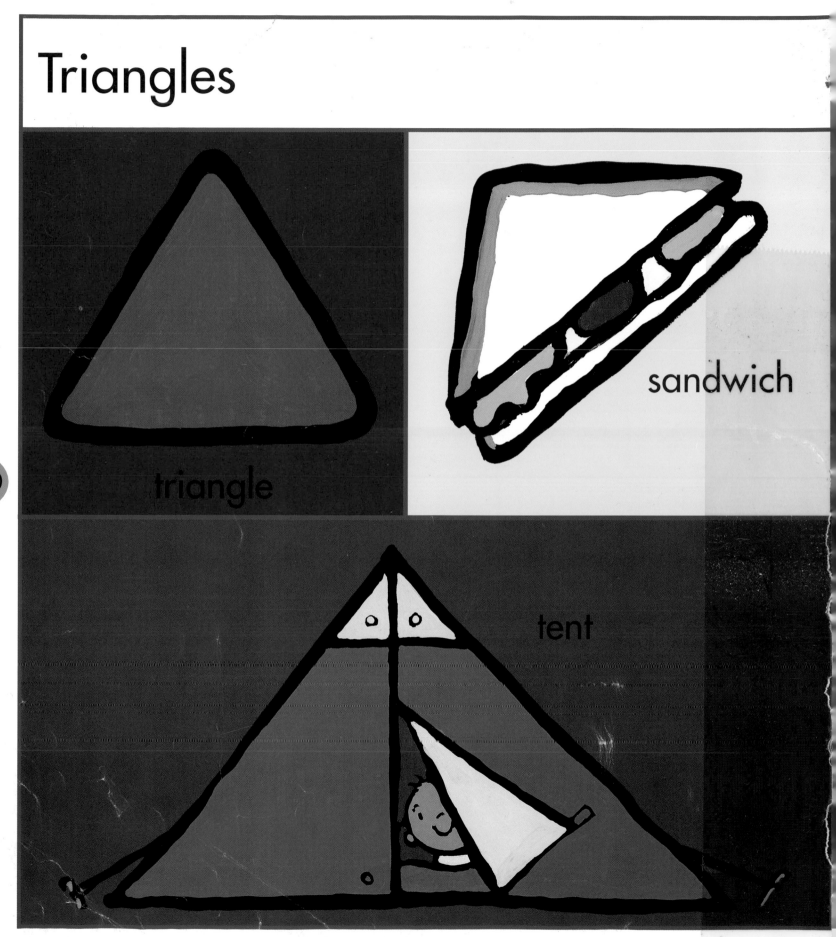

triangle

sandwich

tent

How many triangles can you count on the **tent**?

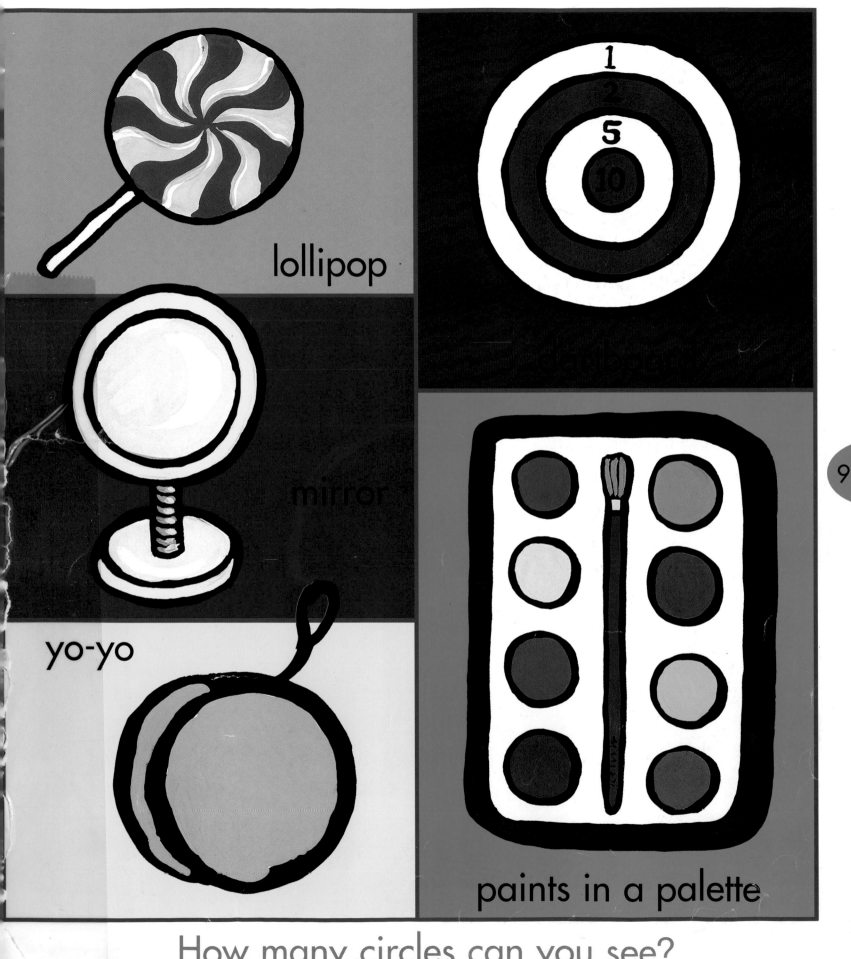

lollipop

mirror

yo-yo

paints in a palette

How many circles can you see?

Circles

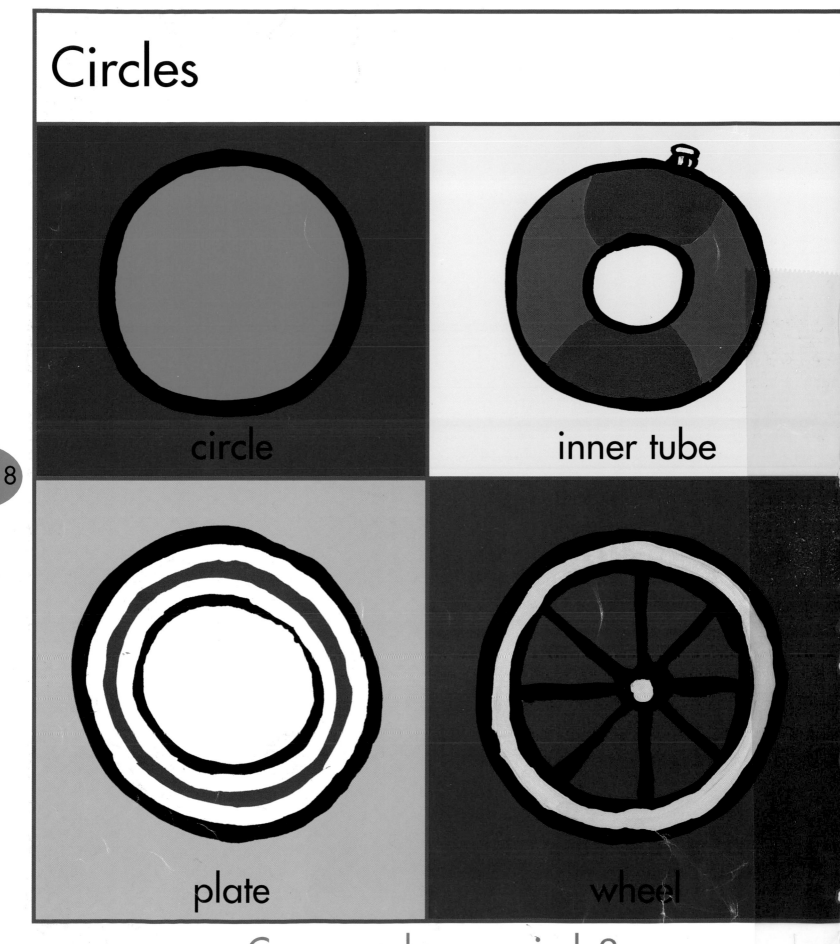

circle

inner tube

plate

wheel

Can you draw a circle?

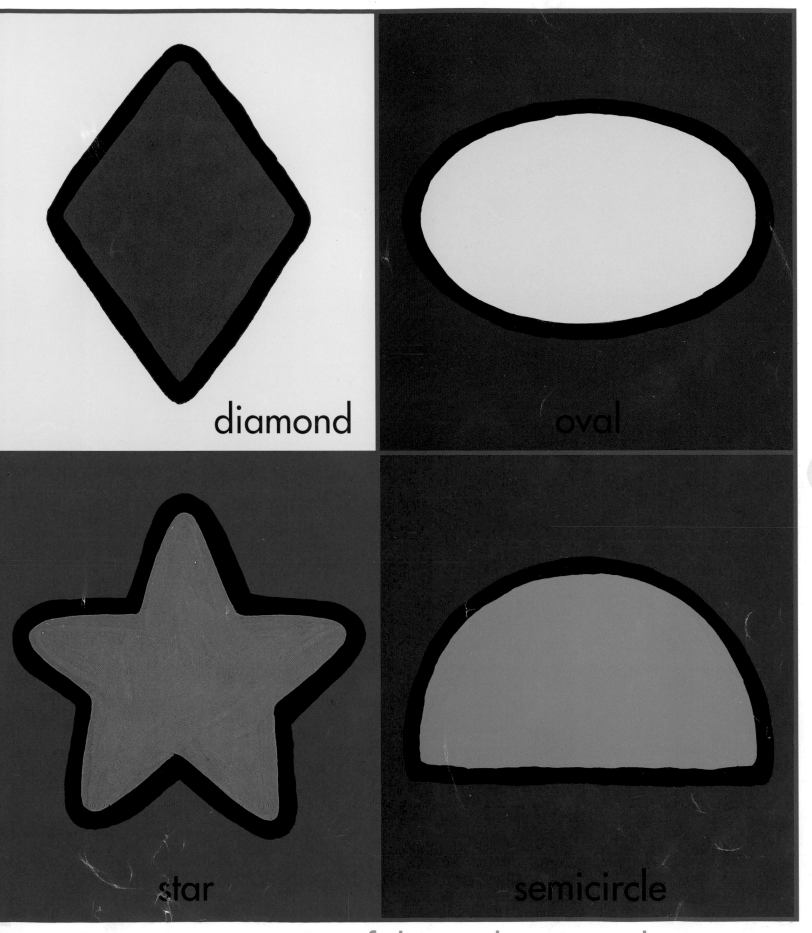

diamond

oval

star

semicircle

Can you see any of these shapes at home?

Meet the shapes

circle

square

triangle

rectangle

Which shapes are green?

they see so that they begin to understand that, although some shapes have the same number of sides, they are not the same shape.

Learning doesn't have to stop when the book is closed! Together, look at things in your home and outside, and identify them by their shape. This book should give you plenty of ideas of what to look for. When out shopping, for example, talk about the shapes of packages, looking for boxes with square faces or the circular ends of tubes. Your child will enjoy using his or her new knowledge when playing with toys, especially those that can be used for building. Talk together about the shapes that can be seen in the faces of building blocks. Make repeating patterns using blocks or other toys, and encourage your child to describe the pattern and say what comes next.

Above all, remember that learning is fun!

Ann Montague-Smith

Ann Montague-Smith, Principal Lecturer in Primary Education
University College Worcester, England

5